# MINDFULNESS FOR BEGINNERS
## IN 10 MINUTES A DAY

D1402360

# MINDFULNESS
## FOR BEGINNERS
### IN 10 MINUTES A DAY

Mindful Moments to Bring Clarity and Calm to
Your Morning, Day, and Night

LARA HOCHEISER

ROCKRIDGE
PRESS

*For Cori. You brought me back to my path. I am grateful for you. I miss you eternally.*

# CONTENTS

# INTRODUCTION

Welcome to your mindfulness journey. Take a deep breath and get comfortable. You have everything you need inside you.

Why are you here? Maybe you tried formal meditation practices and struggled. Maybe you examined your relationship with stress and realized it was time for a change. Maybe you recognized you're having trouble being present and feeling joy in your life. Maybe you are coping with loss and change, and you hope to open your heart again. No matter the impetus, you are in the right place.

I have been practicing yoga and mindfulness since age 17. My early childhood was traumatic, and I attempted to dissociate myself from difficult experiences. I pushed down rejection, pain, and anger. In young adulthood, I struggled to make safe choices and often found myself wondering why my behavior didn't align with my core values. Who was I becoming?

Yoga and mindfulness helped me shape my mind and body. I began to chip away at the fortress I had erected around my heart. I started to feel like my thoughts and actions reflected the truth of who I was inside. Yet, to this day, I struggle with the fight-or-flight impulse when I feel triggered, so I lean on my mindfulness practice to put distance between my impulses to act and my actions.

We can grow and heal ourselves to shift our patterns of thoughts and behaviors throughout our lifetimes. Every moment presents an opportunity to use a kind, gentle mind to examine what we are experiencing without judgment and with curiosity and love. These shifts in mind-set are not permanent. Like a gardener tending to a plot to remove weeds and nourish the harvest, we too must work consistently and incrementally to experience the growth commensurate with that of a garden in full bloom.

Daily practice has a significant impact. When I was in my mid-20s, I was studying yoga and mindfulness and decided I wanted to think more positively. For six months, I journaled for about five minutes per day. I had to write my way back to gratitude no matter how challenging things got. I've felt the positive effects of this practice for years. Now, when I feel my old doom and gloom, I can reach for this practice to bring myself back to positive thinking. You can do the practices in this book in just a few minutes at a time. When you do them consistently, you will notice a big impact on your mind and body. You can come back to the practices that support you anytime you need them.

So what is the deal with mindfulness? Mindfulness, while secular, is derived from Buddhism. It has been practiced in the West since the late 1970s, when Jon Kabat-Zinn developed the Mindfulness-Based Stress Reduction (MBSR) program in a clinical setting, where he gathered empirical evidence that mindfulness practices help practitioners experience life with less reactivity and more equanimity. In this book, you will learn some basic mindfulness activities, along with yoga breathing and pose sequences, to work toward a body and mind that feel like home. Whether you are a beginner or have experience with mindfulness practices, you'll find that the activities in this book can shift your relationship with time, attention, presence, and joy. Grab a journal, a pen, and a warm drink, and let's get started.

# WHAT IS MINDFULNESS?

Mindfulness is about bringing the mind back to the moment when it wanders, and doing so with kindness and curiosity: "Hey, mind, where did you go? Thanks for letting me know you care about that thought. Now, let's return to the intended focus."

Mindfulness can be a mental state of clarity, an awareness of thoughts, feelings, and bodily sensations. It can also refer to a character trait that results in a sense of equanimity, which allows practitioners to become less reactive while remaining openhearted and caring. Mindfulness can also refer to big "M" mindfulness (formal seated meditation), which this book does not cover, as well as little "m" mindfulness, such as establishing intentions, moving your body, journaling, and breathing. This book focuses on these activities.

# WHAT DOES IT MEAN
# TO BE MINDFUL?

Most of us need help learning to shut off our autopilot minds to tap into the present moment. But if your automatic mode is stress, distraction, and/or dissociation (the state of being disconnected from your thoughts, feelings, memories, and surroundings), you might miss the life happening right in front of you. What does mindfulness look like?

Picture someone you love talking about something important to them. Imagine yourself looking at them intently, body turned toward them, actively listening to every word. Your mouth is closed. Your ears and heart are open. How do you think your friend would feel? Do you imagine your compassion and empathy could grow by truly listening? What about your connection to this important person?

Now imagine yourself with your friend again. This time, you are so lost in thought that you can't hear them. You stare at your phone as your loved one's words fall on deaf ears. What might you miss by being caught up in your thoughts? Do you think your lack of presence would impact the flow of conversation? Would your friend feel heard or loved?

Now consider which version of yourself you would rather show up as. I bet you want to be able to listen intently and connect deeply. Learning to be mindful has a lot to do with how we listen and how we experience the world around and inside us.

The upcoming chapters focus on setting attainable goals for creating more mindful experiences in your life. The practices in this book are the baby steps you need to take to live more mindfully, and they can prepare you for a deeper meditation practice (if you want one).

As I mentioned, mindfulness can be a character trait. The more you practice mindfulness, the more your character can shift. But for most of us, for whom it doesn't come so easily, being mindful has more to do with experiencing moments of awareness, connection, and compassion amid the stress, overstimulation, and busyness of our lives.

I am not asking you to sit in silent meditation twice a day. That isn't accessible or practical for most people. Instead, I invite you to come off autopilot for short periods as you explore your five senses, your breath, your body, and your thoughts in a safe, engaging, and gentle way.

# WHAT MINDFULNESS IS NOT

Mindfulness is not about being devoid of judgment. Our minds are judgment- and thought-making machines. Rather than fighting judgment, you can expect to notice judgmental thoughts and just label them as such. Then you will be able to use your clear mind to discern what is really happening.

Mindfulness is not saying yes to everyone all the time. Boundaries go hand in hand with mindfulness. Just because your heart is open doesn't mean you are going to give someone the shirt off your back. You will be more in touch with your needs and be a better advocate for yourself with compassionate communication.

Mindfulness is not a religion. People of any faith (or lack thereof) can practice. It can complement any religion or philosophy. Mindfulness is secular, so you can practice it at work and at school.

Mindfulness is not elitist. All people can practice if they want to experience life in the present moment with an open heart and mind. The practice of mindfulness transcends economic, geographic, racial, and other demographic boundaries.

Mindfulness is not a cure for social ills. People who experience systemic racism and economic hardship, for example, cannot overcome these challenges with mindfulness. Many people need systemic changes to feel safe, secure, and peaceful. Mindfulness is not a magic wand.

Mindfulness is not meant to replace Western medicine. Many people will benefit from an approach that includes mindfulness and mental health care or prescription drugs. Always consult a doctor before discontinuing any medical protocol.

# ON MEDITATION

Meditation is often thought of as the holy grail of mental health. Yet for many people, formal, seated meditation is not helpful or accessible—it's often just too hard to make the space in our lives. Also, if you have experienced trauma, have certain mental health conditions, or simply are not in the right environment, state of mind, or company, meditation may be contraindicated and could be dangerous. If you are interested in deeper forms of meditation, ask a highly qualified meditation teacher or your therapist (or both) if any condition you have makes it inadvisable to practice meditation.

In this book, we will tiptoe into some simple, safe, and accessible meditations. If you're like me, you may feel better doing moving meditations than seated ones. This book has a little bit of everything—movement, journaling, breathing, walking meditation, and more. If you want to delve more deeply into one of these practices after finishing this book, go for it. In the case of more formal meditation, choose your meditation style and teachers wisely. There is a common saying in yoga: "When the student is ready, the teacher will appear." Be on the lookout.

# MINDFULNESS IN YOUR LIFE

When you hear the word "mindfulness," you may imagine a monk sitting motionless and peacefully on a cushion. Although that's a nice visual, you need to remember that most people's lives are busier, more stressful, and more stimulating than a monk's existence at a monastery. Your mindfulness practices can suit your busy lifestyle. Let's take a moment to imagine what that might look like.

What can mindfulness be for you? It can be a deep breath before going into an important work event, the ability to savor a special moment with loved ones, the tools to be fully present despite the myriad challenges and stressors you face, the rituals to wind down at night, or a million other experiences and practices.

Imagine taking the time to savor your first bite of a meal to truly taste the flavors, rather than scarfing down your food. Imagine walking slowly, tapped into all your senses, rather than rushing around lost in thought. Imagine choosing to do short, sweet activities that make your normal life and work more rewarding, engaging, and special. Right now, you have the ability to make tiny changes to enjoy more gratitude, presence, kindness, compassion, and awe every single day.

One of the best parts about this everyday approach to mindfulness is that you can do it quickly and with no prerequisite skills. With a few minutes of practice throughout the day, you can start to enjoy the benefits of calmer, more satisfying mornings; empowering, present, energizing days; and relaxing, fulfilling nights.

Busyness doesn't preclude you from enjoying a rich life right now. Through the use of breath, journaling, embodied movement, attentional activities, affirmations, and acts of kindness, we will explore little "m" mindfulness. I have outlined more than 50 easy-to-do activities that will each take you 10 minutes or less. Choose the ones that feel right for you and make them regular, daily practices. You *can* do this. When you make this commitment to yourself, you will see your work, your relationships with yourself and others, and your mind begin to transform. There is no time like the present.

2

# MINDFUL MORNINGS

Mindfulness can seem out of reach when we are struggling with anxiety, depression, low energy, and other challenges. Mornings are an ideal time to practice mindfulness for this reason. It helps train your mind and body to crave positive, meaningful, and gentle activities that give you a chance to get the most out of each day.

Enjoy more mindful moments in the morning by choosing the practices from this chapter that resonate with you. Repeat them often (most days, if you can) to establish a morning routine that supports living your life with presence and equanimity. A feeling of steadiness mixed with positive thinking, gentle movement, and breathing can make a world of difference. Let's explore some options you can combine in a unique way to live the life you've been longing for from sunrise to sunset.

# Waking Up Grateful

🕐 TIME: 1–2 MINUTES

Gratitude is one of the practices of gladdening the mind. This concept is taught by psychologist and mindfulness teacher Tara Brach. To start the day with a glad mind, let's take a journey into gratitude together. I invite you to try this activity with a reasonable dose of skepticism. You may need to go through the motions a few times before you have the experience of truly feeling gratitude, and that's okay.

First, let go of any anxiety that you don't have enough time. You deserve to experience the benefits of this practice. If you are worried that closing your eyes first thing in the morning isn't practical, consider this: Is it practical to start your morning stressed out about what's to come and carry that feeling into your day? Or is it a better idea to set the tone for your day inside your mind and heart in two minutes or less?

1. When you wake up, keep your eyes closed. (Okay, okay, you may need to shut off your alarm or bring a wiggling child into bed with you, but then close your eyes again.)

2. Take a deep breath. As you inhale gently through your nose, feel your belly expand.

3. As you exhale through your mouth, whisper, "Thank you." You may choose to picture people and anything else that makes your life beautiful as you do so. It is key to slow down the exhale, so take your time.

4. Repeat these steps 5 to 10 times, or until the practice feels complete. Notice how you feel.

TIP: *You may choose to jot down in your journal how this practice impacts you to become aware of changes from day to day. The depth of gratitude deepens as your heart opens, and this practice is just one that can help you.*

# Getting the Kinks Out

⏱ TIME: 5–10 MINUTES

Make your morning stretch an opportunity to prepare your mind and body for the new day ahead. You will need a clear spot to stretch as well as a yoga mat, sturdy rug, or beach towel.

As you roll out your mat or smooth your rug or towel, draw your attention to the textures you feel and the colors you see. Remind yourself that there is nothing to accomplish. These movements are intended to sweeten your day. You will be doing a sequence from tabletop to child's pose back to tabletop and then on to cow and cat pose. If you are short on time, you can do one or the other.

### STEP-BY-STEP GUIDE FOR TABLETOP INTO CHILD'S POSE

1. Come to your hands and knees with your shoulders over your wrists and hips over your knees. Spread out your fingers and press firmly into your palms. Notice the sensations in your body. Take a deep breath in.

2. Next, widen your knees, bring your big toes toward one another, and rock your hips back, allowing them to land on or near your heels.

3. Come into child's pose by walking your palms forward and slowly lowering your chest and forehead as you keep your hips down. Breathe out. If you can't place your forehead on the floor, stack your hands and place your forehead on them. You may notice your nervous system start to relax.

4. After a few deep breaths in child's pose, come back to tabletop pose.

### STEP-BY-STEP GUIDE FOR TABLETOP INTO COW AND CAT POSE

1. Press firmly into your hands in tabletop position. Breathe in as you lower your belly and draw your chest forward. This action should broaden your chest. Look forward or up, whichever feels right for your neck. This is cow pose.

2. As you breathe out, round your upper back and look to your navel. This action should broaden and round your upper back. You may be able to suck your belly in toward your spine as you exhale. Don't worry if you can't do so right away. This is cat pose.

3. Alternate poses several times as you breathe slowly.

4. When you feel complete, note how your body feels. If you want to do any other stretches or movements, give yourself another moment to complete them.

# Brushing with Presence

To distinguish between the autopilot approach to tooth-brushing and a conscious, present, and even elated variation, first consider how you normally brush your teeth. Do you focus singularly on brushing, or are you thinking about other things? Are you using all your senses to experience the feelings of toothbrushing? What are you doing with your eyes and ears? In this practice, you will employ all your senses and expand your conscious awareness.

## STEP-BY-STEP GUIDE

1. Come to the sink. Stand with your hips square to the sink and mirror. Mentally note, "I am going to brush my teeth with my full attention."

2. Pick up your toothbrush. Notice how it looks and feels.

3. Rinse your toothbrush. Note its appearance. Listen to the water run.

4. Turn off the water, and as you apply toothpaste, notice if you can smell the toothpaste. If you can, what does the sensation feel like in your nose? Does the scent remind you of anything?

5. Once you're ready to brush, run your tongue over your teeth and note the taste in your mouth.

6. Spend a few seconds brushing each surface of each tooth. Do you make little circles or go back and forth? Do you have a method or process you always follow? If you do, simply noting it can take you out of autopilot and into presence. Do you feel a particular sensation as you brush? What does it feel like? Label the sensations using neutral language.

7. As you brush, you may choose to look at yourself in the mirror. If you do, watch yourself and ask, "Do I appear to be paying close attention to this task?"

8. Once you are done brushing each tooth, rinse your mouth and listen to the sounds. Notice the sensations of the water as you rinse. Spit out the excess fluid.

9. Run your tongue across your teeth again. Note the difference between the start and end of this practice.

10. Put your brushing items away neatly. With a feeling of gratitude for your attention, mentally thank yourself and note that this activity is done: "Thank you. This is complete."

# Grounding Down

This practice can help you transition into your morning activities feeling empowered and connected. Being grounded translates to a secure sense of being tethered to the earth. You can feel this connection physically through the sense of touch and energetically through a palpable sense of security.

You can ground yourself inside or outside. Over time, you can sense when you are complete, but when starting out, you may want to set a timer for a few minutes.

### STEP-BY-STEP GUIDE FOR INSIDE

1. Choose a flat place to stand, such as a carpet, yoga mat, or tile floor.

2. If you are in a serene space, you can keep your eyes open. If you must choose a distracting place, you may want to close your eyes. If you keep them open, let your eyes be gentle (that is, relax your eyelids and gaze). You can always choose to close your eyes or keep them open.

3. Bring your attention into your feet. Feel the connection between your feet and the ground. Notice where your feet and the floor make contact. Notice the negative space between your feet and the floor.

4. Imagine grounding your feet, like tree roots, firmly through the ground. Your sense of stability can go deeper than the surface. Visualize and embody the grounded feeling of a deeply rooted tree.

5. Once complete, take a moment to notice how you feel.

## STEP-BY-STEP GUIDE FOR OUTSIDE

1. Choose a flat place to stand, such as grass, mud, dirt, or moss. If weather permits and you feel comfortable doing so, take off your shoes.

2. Find a place ahead of you on which to steady your gaze with your eyes gently open. Or you may close your eyes if you wish.

3. Notice the sensation of the contact points of your feet and the ground. If your shoes are off, pay attention to the textures, temperature, and other tactile information you receive through your feet. (You may feel these sensations with shoes on, too, but less intensely.) Notice the negative space between your feet and the earth.

4. Imagine grounding your feet firmly, like a tree's deep roots. Visualizing the image of your roots can be helpful in forming a sense of security.

5. Once complete, take a moment to notice how you feel.

# Invigorating Morning Flow

🕐 TIME: 5–10 MINUTES

Low on energy? Perhaps you can skip a second cup of coffee and instead give yourself the gift of natural energy and alertness with a half sun salutation, which is perfect for beginners. Don't worry if you can't touch your toes yet; this sequence doesn't need to be perfect. If you know the whole sun salutation, feel free to add on. Do this series on a yoga mat, carpet, or towel.

## STEP-BY-STEP GUIDE

1.  Mountain pose: Stand up tall. Bend your knees slightly. Lengthen your spine by lifting your sternum (just atop your heart) and the crown of your head toward the ceiling. Put some weight into your tailbone. Bring your palms together in front of your heart. As you press your hands together, broaden your chest and back. Inhale. As you exhale, bring your navel to your spine. As you inhale again, reach your arms up and look up.

2.  Ragdoll pose: As you exhale, bend your knees and fold forward. Allow your hands to drop, then grab your opposite elbows. Let your legs bend so much that you can rest your belly on your thighs. Let your head drop

and look toward your belly. As you breathe in, lift your butt higher toward the ceiling; as you breathe out, bend your knees a bit more and lengthen your chest down your legs toward your knees, eventually releasing your head again at the top of your exhale.

3. Flat back pose: As you breathe in, bend your knees. Bring your hands to your knees or thighs as you lengthen your spine forward and bring your butt back. Keep your neck long by tucking in your chin slightly. Do not allow your ribs to splay open, which results in your belly bulging out; rather, gently firm your belly and imagine a gentle corset keeping your ribs neutral. If you were to look in the mirror, your back would be flat, not curved.

4. Ragdoll pose: As you exhale, fold forward again. Allow your back to lengthen and release on the inhales and exhales.

5. Mountain pose: Bend your knees slightly and come through your flat back again. As you lengthen your spine, keep your belly firm to protect your spine. Slowly stand up by pressing firmly down into your feet. Once you are standing tall, bring your palms together at your heart. Notice how you feel.

6. Complete this sequence 5 to 10 times to warm your body or repeat as many times as you wish.

# Breathing Through the Nose

🕐 TIME: 1–5 MINUTES

A smooth breath can help you feel calm, energized, and safe. For many, learning to smooth out the breath takes regular practice, so don't worry if you need to try this technique many times before your breath gets really smooth and soothing.

Some keys to smooth breath are gently closed lips and a slight constriction in the throat. How do you constrict the throat? Tuck in your chin a bit and swallow. Now start inhaling and exhaling through your nostrils. If you have any issues breathing through your nostrils, you may substitute by breathing through your mouth. Keep water handy to quench any dryness.

This breathing practice is super simple. Over time, you can take longer inhales and exhales. You can aim for about 2 seconds at first, and over time get to 5 to 10 seconds for each breath.

1. Find a comfortable seated position with your spine tall, perhaps in a chair, seated upright on the floor, or on a cushion. If it feels tiring, don't worry. It will get easier with practice.

2. Gently close your lips and let your tongue sit on the roof of your mouth.

3. Inhale slowly through your nose. Make the breath as quiet and smooth as you can. If you'd like, you can add a short pause here, holding in the breath, before moving on to the next step. As you pause, relax your face and shoulders.

4. Exhale slowly through your nose. Again, make the breath as quiet and smooth as you can. You can add a short pause here before taking in another breath.

5. Continue breathing this way until you feel complete.

# Journaling for a Great Day

Early in the day is a wonderful time to take the reins of your attitude and intention. Steer your mind using your pen. This activity doesn't have to take a lot of time. Journaling about how you want your day to feel and what you want to focus on and accomplish can help you set yourself up for success. Grab your pen and your journal and respond to these prompts:

### Journal Prompts Option 1

> How do I want to feel today?

> What kinds of experiences help me feel this way?

> What might I do to try to experience these feelings?

### Journal Prompts Option 2

> What is my intention for the day?

> To whom do I dedicate my day?

> How do I want to spend my time today?

*I've heard within my inmost soul*
*Such cheerful morning news,*
*In the horizon of my mind*
*Have seen such orient hues,*

*As in the twilight of the dawn,*
*When the first birds awake,*
*Are heard within some silent wood,*
*Where they the small twigs break,*

*Or in the eastern skies are seen,*
*Before the sun appears,*
*The harbingers of summer heats*
*Which from afar he bears.*

—Excerpt from "The Inward Morning"
by Henry David Thoreau

# Walking Mindfully

🕐 TIME: 1–10 MINUTES (OR MORE IF AVAILABLE)

Did you know the quality of attention you bring into how you walk can result in more joy and presence and help you escape from mindless thinking or worrying? Try walking to start your day. In this exercise, you'll bring your attention to the sensation in your feet, the weight shifting as your body moves, and the sensory information you take in as you move.

You can do this indoors or outside. Space constraints might limit you to walking up and down a hallway, in circles around a room, or in some other creative way. It's okay if you don't have a ton of room. Pay attention to the space as you walk. If you can get outside, choose a spot in the distance to walk toward. You can walk mindfully across the yard, for miles and miles on a hike, or simply across the street. Wherever you go, move with mindful attention, noticing the sights and scents of nature as well as human-made things around you.

1. Stand up mindfully. Slowly set your gaze on something on the horizon.

2. Step one foot forward. Go slowly and place your foot down heel to toe. When your toes touch down, step your other foot forward, heel to toe.

3. As you move in this conscious way, feel the sensation of your feet on the floor or the ground. Notice the sensation of your weight shifting as you place your foot and when you step on your other foot.

4. Notice what you see, hear, smell, and feel as you mindfully place one foot in front of the other. If you get lost in thought, gently return your attention to your senses and the methodical way you are walking.

# Taking a Mindful Seat

⏱ TIME: 2 MINUTES

Sitting mindfully is a great way to combat poor posture and bring your mind fully into the present. Slouching can cause fatigue and muscle weakness, and gives others the impression that you aren't listening. Upright, or mindful, posture helps your mind feel alert and calm, aligns your bones so your muscles are gently working, and signals to others that you are present.

You can sit mindfully in a chair or on the floor. If you take a mindful seat on the floor, you will need a yoga block, cushion, or folded towel to sit on. Although the posture looks simple, sitting upright takes core strength, which can be a challenge to many people. Be patient with yourself. If you are just starting out, you can use a timer and try sitting this way for two minutes or even for just a few seconds at a time until you build up stamina. If you have more experience, you can sit for as long as you'd like.

## STEP-BY-STEP GUIDE FOR CHAIR

1. Set up a sturdy chair, preferably without wheels.

2. Sit as you normally would and notice your posture and feeling of alertness for a few moments. Stand up.

3. Sit in the chair again. This time, sit forward so you are not leaning on the back.

4. Place your knees in alignment over your ankles, and press your feet firmly into the floor. Press your palms into your thighs to help you sit up tall.

5. Once upright, intentionally lengthen your waist and the back of your neck.

6. After a few minutes, notice your posture and alertness again.

## STEP-BY-STEP GUIDE FOR FLOOR

1. Sit cross-legged on the floor and place a yoga block, cushion, or folded towel under the bony part of your bottom, not your whole seat. If your knees are up high or you can't sit up tall, you will need a taller object to sit on. Ideally, you want your knees lower than your hips.

2. Make sure you feel steady. Notice your posture and feeling of alertness. Press your palms into your knees to help you sit up taller.

3. Once upright, intentionally lengthen your spine, the sides of your waist, and your neck.

4. After a few minutes, notice your posture and alertness again.

# Charting Your Free Time

It can be frustrating when the new mindful habits you are trying to integrate into your day fall by the wayside and vices and distractions take up the majority of your free time. One way to pull yourself out of a bad-habit loop is to visualize your free time by creating a pie chart of your wanted behaviors in your journal before you start your day. If you want, you can get creative and color-code your chart. You don't have to take away any unwanted behaviors, but adding healthy, intentional ones will cause the less savory ones to diminish.

1. In your journal, draw a circle. Above it write, "My Free Time."

2. Split the circle into pie slices, showing what percentage of your free time you want to spend in different ways. Some examples may be *breathing intentionally, moving, spending time with my kids, spending time alone, spending time in nature, hiking, playing, telling jokes, reading, writing, calling a loved one,* and *doing charitable works.* If you know the structure of your day, you can get really specific with the activities.

3. Beneath your chart, you can write down how many minutes each free-time activity gets. You can even add these activities to your calendar or tasks for the day.

4. In the evening, reflect on how you spent your time. Don't worry if you didn't do it all perfectly. You can try again each day, and little by little add more of your desired mindful behaviors to the chart.

# Centering

Centering is connecting to your internal experience. You get a chance to notice what is happening inside you without judgment. You'll sit still, noticing your thoughts, emotions, and bodily sensations. You may want to fidget. You may be thinking about your day. All that is okay. You will simply return your attention to your inward focus, then spend a few moments observing your breath. This exercise is not fancy. You do not need to feel calm, but sitting this way usually leads you to feel calm and centered.

Centering can also be part of observing the world around you and taking it in through your senses by fixing your gaze on a single point and zooming out your focus to notice the colors, objects, sounds, lighting, smells, and other observable phenomena in a space. This kind of centering can help you prepare to face the world around you.

You may want to center both ways, by first turning inward and then outward, or simply choose one if you are pressed for time. I recommend doing this practice while sitting comfortably in a chair or on the floor.

## STEP-BY-STEP GUIDE FOR CENTERING INTERNALLY

1. Close your eyes and turn your focus inward.

2. Notice your thoughts for 60 seconds.

3. Shift your focus to your emotions for 60 seconds.

4. Shift your focus to your bodily sensations. Scan from your head to your toes for as long as it takes.

5. Once you have noticed your thoughts, emotions, and sensations, spend a moment observing your gentle breath.

6. After about five minutes, notice how you feel.

## STEP-BY-STEP GUIDE FOR CENTERING EXTERNALLY

1. Open your eyes. Keep your gaze relaxed and comfortable.

2. Looking forward, take in as much as you can, noting how far you can see peripherally as well as up and down.

3. Silently name the objects and colors you see.

4. Note any smells, sounds, and sensations. You may mentally note what you smell, hear, and feel.

5. Once you have taken in the space around you, spend a moment observing your gentle breath.

6. After about five minutes, notice how you feel.

# Showering Sensually

How do you normally go about bathing? Do you pay keen attention to the sensations, smells, and other sensory information, or do you just get clean? Try a mindful shower, in which you allow yourself to experience the full range of sensuality your body can experience. (If you take baths, you can apply the same principles.)

When I taught mindful hand washing during a workshop, a participant said she had an orgasmic experience from washing her hands! Another told me she had a sensual experience that she could not believe was available just by paying closer attention. I hope your interest is piqued.

## STEP-BY-STEP GUIDE

1. Turn on the water. As it adjusts to the desired temperature, say to yourself, "I am going to have a sensual shower."

2. As you disrobe, notice the feeling of the air on your skin. Does your skin react in any way? Tune in to that sensory experience.

3. Place your hand under the running water and check if the temperature feels pleasant. Bring all your awareness into your hand as the water runs over it.

4. Step into the shower stall. Allow your head to come under the stream of water. The top of your head is a sensitive part of the body. If possible, close your eyes as you wet your hair. How does your scalp react?

5. Using the same level of attention, wash each body part one at a time. Notice the sensations and smells as you wash. As you breathe in and out, can you feel the steam in your lungs? What does it feel like?

6. Once you have rinsed off, mentally state, "I am done with my sensual shower." Take a moment to reflect on some of your experiences, perhaps noting mentally, "It felt surprisingly good when I rinsed my hair."

7. As you towel off, take a moment to express gratitude to yourself for taking a sensual shower. You can use the same level of awareness as you moisturize or brush your hair.

8. Have a great day or a wonderful evening!

# Building and Keeping Your Sanctuary

As you embark on your mindful journey, you will want to establish a place in your home that feels like a sanctuary—for prayer, meditation, and/or centering and connecting deeply. It can be as small as a tabletop or even a shoebox, a traditional altar, an entire room, a wall of shelves, or anything else. You can spend 10 minutes each day setting up your sanctuary. Once it's complete, you can use it as a place to sit, clear your mind, and do your mindfulness activities.

Your sanctuary can be as elaborate or as simple as you want. You do not need to spend a lot of money to create a serene space. Arrange your sanctuary with items that invite you in a calm and alluring way. Consider these items, all of which smell, feel, look, or sound beautiful:

> Stones, crystals, rocks, and other natural minerals

> Feathers

> Cleansing herbs or incense, such as sage, palo santo, or copal, which can be burned or spritzed from a spray bottle, depending on what is best for you and your space

- Photos, images, or statues of people or deities/gods you are devoted to

- Fabric to line the surface of your altar

- Plants

- A journal and pen that call you to write

- A chime, bell, or other resonant instrument (these don't have to be expensive)

- A yoga mat, meditation cushion, or something else to sit on

On nature walks, keep your eyes peeled for some of these items. There is no need to put financial pressure on yourself; you can purchase other items over time. Make sure everything you choose appeals to your senses. You know you've done a good job on your sanctuary space if, upon seeing it, you are called to practice mindfulness.

Your sanctuary can be an ever-changing place for you to land and center. Listen to your inner voice calling you to rearrange, change out objects, or make the space simpler or more elaborate. Keep the surface clean. Let the objects in your sanctuary get regular sunlight to recharge them with the magical healing powers of the earth's only star. Honor your sanctuary as a sacred space. If you have kids, make sure they respect the space, too.

# Setting Intentions

An intention is a heart-centered focus that you intend to work toward for a designated period. Because it's an intention rather than a goal, goal-oriented people can have a hard time grasping this concept. Worry not. You can look at intention as a goal you set with your heart.

You may have heard a yoga teacher ask you to set an intention for your practice but not known exactly what to do. Your intention can be to focus on your breath throughout a practice, to connect deeply with a friend or loved one when they are speaking, or to be present throughout your day. Notice how each of these intentions has a short, designated time frame.

I recommend stating your intention three or more times, mentally or aloud (if appropriate). State your intention in present tense, rather than future tense. For example, instead of saying "I will focus on my breath throughout this practice," say "I am focusing on my breath throughout this practice" or "I am focused on my breath throughout this practice."

When you speak or think your intention, do so with gratitude in your heart, as if it has already come true. Using the present tense helps you feel that you are already the change you are becoming. You are the future self you are building with attention and intention in the present moment. Your changes, although they happen over time and can feel subtle, are also occurring right now. Your mind and behavior can be shaped by your intention. This is wonderful because your mind and behavior can begin to mirror whatever resides inside your heart. You are loving and good. You have the attention to focus on your intention for a short period.

## STEP-BY-STEP GUIDE

1. Take a mindful seat (see "Taking a Mindful Seat," page 26). Close your eyes.

2. Express a feeling of gratitude, even if you have to fake it at first. For some guidance, see "Waking Up Grateful" on page 10.

3. Notice what is in your heart, and find a positive phrase for voicing your intention.

4. Mentally or aloud, repeat your intention three times in the present tense, and notice how you feel.

TIP: *Practice setting intention regularly at the same time each day, perhaps before you do one of your other mindfulness activities.*

# Asking Better
# Self-Inquiry Questions

⏱ TIME: 5–10 MINUTES

The morning is a superb time to reflect on the day ahead. Self-inquiry is an amazing part of a mindfulness practice and can help us escape the hamster wheel of automaticity. Sometimes we go on autopilot, where we move through the must-dos of our day without slowing down to ask ourselves how we want our day to go and how we want to feel. When we ask ourselves better questions, we don't just make a to-do list, we make a *to-be* list.

### STEP-BY-STEP GUIDE

1. Grab your notebook and pen. Take a mindful seat at your sanctuary or in a peaceful place (see "Taking a Mindful Seat," page 26). Close your eyes, or keep your eyes gently open, and go inside yourself.

2. With your awareness, first note how you are feeling. Mentally label what you notice, being sure not to judge anything as good or bad, right or wrong. Your feelings just are.

3. Ask yourself, "How do I want to feel today?" Wait for the answer to come.

4. Once you get your answer, open your journal and list the things you like to do that help you feel that way. (Tip: Don't make a list of things that are impossible or unattainable; choose easy-to-achieve tasks, such as reaching out to a loved one or spending five minutes doing something creative, so you won't feel over-whelmed or defeated.)

5. Consider when in your day you can make time to help yourself pause and mindfully take action to experience the contentment, satisfaction, joy, connection, or other emotion you are seeking.

6. Make a plan to fit your desired tasks into your regular schedule.

TIP: *The items on my to-be list are nonnegotiable, and I put them into my work calendar because they are as important as work tasks for making me productive, focused, and engaged. If a written schedule is not for you, think of ways to structure your day to do more of the things that will help you feel content and whole.*

# Devoting Your Attention

The morning is an opportunity to go inward *and* reflect outwardly on the world around you. By scanning your inner experience with your awareness and using your senses to observe the outside world, you can welcome the new day. This is a two-part exercise. You may want to start by doing one part at a time. As you improve your ability to sustain your attention, do both. Each part takes about five minutes.

## STEP-BY-STEP GUIDE FOR INWARD REFLECTION

1. Take a mindful seat, perhaps at your altar or sanctuary (see "Taking a Mindful Seat," page 26).

2. Tune in to your natural breath by closing your eyes and observing the sounds and sensations of breath entering and leaving your body. Perhaps the sensations most prominent are in your nostrils and belly.

3. Scan your body from your head to your toes. Notice the sensations in your body, such as pulsation, warmth, rigidity, or fluidness. Note whether you are labeling these as good or bad, and instead simply note the sensation rather than giving it a value. If possible, use

neutral language, such as "sharp sensation" rather than "pain."

4. Note your mental state. How busy is your mind? How distant or close are your thoughts?

5. Note your emotional state. You may choose to label this as well, such as mentally stating, "I notice I am feeling anxious/happy/peaceful."

6. Continue for five minutes, then move on to outward reflection, if desired.

## STEP-BY-STEP GUIDE FOR OUTWARD REFLECTION

1. Slowly open your eyes.

2. If you are near a window, observe the world outside. If not, perhaps step outdoors.

3. Note any wildlife you can hear or see.

4. Note any sounds you can hear.

5. Take in the sky. Is the sun out? Can you see clouds?

6. After two to three minutes of observing the world around you, notice again how you feel.

7. If you'd like, spend two to three minutes journaling about your experience.

# Savoring the First Sip

Most people enjoy a hot beverage in the morning, but this experience can become automatic over time. If you are brewing tea or coffee, you can extend your mindful attention to the preparation process—seing and smelling the brew, and noticing how your body anticipates the beverage. Use your full attention in the preparation process.

1. Once you're ready to drink your warm beverage, take a seat at a table.

2. Look closely at your drink. Can you see steam rising off the top? What's happening inside your mouth as you delay drinking?

3. Take a big sniff of your drink. Notice how the vapors feel in your nose.

4. When you are ready, take a slow sip. If it's not too hot, keep the liquid in your mouth a little longer than usual. Employ your taste buds to take note of the flavor.

5. Notice how long you can feel the drink in your mouth, and when you decide to swallow, notice when you can no longer feel the liquid in your mouth and throat. Pause before taking another sip.

TIP: *You can drink your whole beverage this way, tapping into the flavors and sensations the whole mug through.*

# Observing the Sounds Around You

🕐 TIME: 10 MINUTES

In this seated meditation, you will be tuning in to the sounds in your orbit. Because you have had some practice focusing your mind and getting centered, you can be confident about trying this activity now. The first few times you may do this for just 2 or 3 minutes before working your way up to 10.

1. Take a mindful seat on a cushion, chair, or park bench (see "Taking a Mindful Seat," page 26). Set your timer.

2. Close your eyes and turn inward.

3. Tune in to your sense of hearing (you might even imagine your ears perking up).

4. Listen to the sounds happening all around you. Notice where the sounds are originating. Take note if and when they cease. Play with listening to sounds nearby and far away, high and low, outside and inside you.

5. When your timer sounds, take a moment to notice how you feel. Perhaps jot down the effects of your practice in your journal, then mindfully return to your life.

3

# MINDFUL DAYS

If your days are busy and packed with obligations, life may feel like one stressor after another. Taking a short break to be mindful can transport your mind and body back to the present moment. When you learn to channel your energy fully into the present, replenish your energy sources and confidence, and reflect on what is going on right now, your quality of life improves.

Break up your busy day with these quick mindfulness activities. Repeat your favorites often. Aim to create a personal daily practice that suits the life you're currently living. Trust yourself to find the ideal mindfulness activities that work for you right now, and allow your personal practice to develop naturally.

# Pausing

⏻ TIME: 2-3 MINUTES

Working, studying, parenting, or anything else your day holds can become overwhelming. A little mindful pause goes a long way toward increasing feelings of empathy and compassion. Anytime you need to slow down and get steady, heart-centered, and focused, try this heart and belly breath. You can do this practice at your desk, outside on a bench, or at your sanctuary whenever you need to slow down.

1. Take a mindful seat (see "Taking a Mindful Seat," page 26). Close your eyes and turn inward. Notice how you are feeling.

2. Place one warm, heavy hand on your heart and the other hand on your lower belly. Relax your belly, but make sure to stay seated upright—not too rigid and not too relaxed, but gently alert.

3. Feel the warmth of your hands connecting with your body. Begin to breathe the smooth, relaxed, slightly constricted breaths you practiced in the morning activities (see "Breathing Through the Nose" on page 20).

4. Take 10 to 15 breaths. Each inhale and exhale should be 2 to 4 seconds, slowly lengthening as you continue breathing. You might find yourself breathing in and out for much longer than 4 seconds.

5. Once you complete the breaths, keep your eyes gently closed and your hands firmly on your body. Notice again how you are feeling, then return to your day.

# Getting Up to Stretch

⏱ TIME: 4 MINUTES

If you spent your morning toiling away—whether on household chores, parenting, work, studies, or some combination of activities—your body has likely fallen into an unconscious posture. I notice some signs when my body wants me to get up and stretch. What signs does your body give you that it needs a moment of movement? Do you get neck pain? Do you start to fidget? What is your body trying to tell you, and do you listen?

You might want to set an alarm to go off at noon as a reminder to get up, stretch, and walk around. Otherwise, you can use the signals from your body to make it official: it's time to stretch. For the most benefits, do both the crescent moon and the lunge.

## STEP-BY-STEP GUIDE FOR THE CRESCENT MOON

1. Stand up with your feet hip-width apart or with your big toes touching and heels slightly apart.

2. Reach your arms up and clasp your hands with your palms touching. Release your index fingers and point them upward to make a steeple.

3. As you inhale, stretch as tall as you can, lengthening your arms and squeezing your elbows in by your ears.

4. As you exhale, stretch your arms overhead in an arc to the left and push your hips out to the right, leaving your chest and hips facing forward and making the shape of a crescent moon with your body.

5. Come back to center, lengthening again, and repeat on the other side.

6. Repeat on each side 5 to 10 times.

## STEP-BY-STEP GUIDE FOR THE LUNGE

1. Kneel on a yoga mat, rug, or folded towel.

2. Step your right foot forward, aligning your right knee over your right ankle with your toes pointing straight ahead.

3. Place your hands on the floor shoulder-width distance ahead of your feet to stabilize yourself (you may need to use a yoga block). Peek back to make sure your left hip is aligned over your left knee, forming a 90-degree angle.

*continues* ▶

4.  Once you are aligned and stable, bring both hands to your right thigh, and use this added stability to lengthen your spine.

5.  Press your hands into your thigh to broaden your chest and further lengthen your spine. Press your right palm firmly into your right thigh and massage from mid-thigh toward your knee, as though you are ironing out your quadricep muscle. Repeat the massage as many times as you wish.

6.  Breathe and send your awareness into the left hip flexor (the front of your left hip, where you should feel the stretch). If you need more stretch, place your hands down to frame your front right foot and gently take your left knee back to increase the angle from a right angle to an obtuse angle. Do not make the posture too big; you want to balance a sense of stretch with a firm stability.

7.  After about 10 breaths, repeat the sequence on the other side.

*I have had my dream—like others—*
*and it has come to nothing, so that*
*I remain now carelessly*
*with feet planted on the ground*
*and look up at the sky—*
*feeling my clothes about me,*
*the weight of my body in my shoes,*
*the rim of my hat, air passing in and out*
*at my nose—and decide to dream no more.*

———————————

—"Thursday"
by William Carlos Williams

# Clearing Away Distractions

🕐 TIME: 2–3 MINUTES

Do you ever feel like your environment *and* your mind are both major distractions? For example, you may have a messy desk and lots of thoughts running through your head. A clear work area and a clear mind can be key to feeling better. Anyone can do this activity; I do it with children as young as age four as well as with clients who hold high-level executive jobs. It's all about naming and encapsulating the one thing you are doing, and doing only that until it's complete. With this exercise, all your energy is mindfully channeled into that one task.

1. Prepare your mind and environment for the task you are doing in a calm, clear, purposeful way by naming the activity and putting away anything unrelated to that task to help reduce anxiety and distraction. This might mean closing all extra web browsers and having only one tab open for the one task you need to do online. It may mean cleaning up your desk to have only one textbook on it before the next class. It can mean putting away your sanctuary so you can focus on work.

2. Whatever you are doing, do it fully. The space around you, the objects you are looking at (whether digital or physical), and your mind are crystal clear and focused on this single task. Give yourself time to learn *not* to multitask. Bask in the beauty of focus.

3. When the task is complete, mentally acknowledge this fact by stating in your head, "*(Fill in the blank)* is done." Clear your space of all objects pertaining to this task.

4. Take a moment to breathe and sit with gratitude for what you have just completed. Pause and take 5 to 10 breaths. Note your mental state. Then prepare for your next task.

# Adopting a "Just This" Attitude Online

TIME: 10 MINUTES

Take a mindful seat (see "Taking a Mindful Seat," page 26) and reflect on what it feels like to do work online. Do you feel focused or distracted? Is your attention pulled in different directions, or does it stay on the task at hand? Think of a time you were in a state of focused, creative flow. How did your screen look? Now remember a time you were distracted online. How did your screen look? How did these two screens differ?

Changing your behavior online can be challenging because it's the job of app developers and online marketers to affect your online behavior and pull your attention (and money) in their direction. Here are a few ways to start developing a "just this" attitude:

> Name and notice your distraction to increase your awareness. Mentally state, "This looks interesting. I am going to click it." Eventually you will notice that you want to be pulled away but choose to remain focused by declining tempting distractions.

> To strengthen your focus, keep only one window open in your browser at a time.

> Turn off all notifications.

- Mentally repeat "Just this" to emphasize your singular point of focus.

- If you need to open files and other windows as part of your task, gather only what you need and avoid getting pulled away from the original task. With practice, you will feel a mindful shift from getting lost in the scroll to feeling in control.

- Periodically remind yourself of what you are working on, using a visual reminder, a written list, or an automatic reminder from your phone or virtual assistant.

- For at least one week, say this mantra to yourself every time you open your computer: "I am in control of my attention."

Take a few minutes to respond to these journal prompts:

- What distracts me when I am working online?

- Do I feel that I am using my time well when I am on internet-connected devices? If so, in which ways? If not, why not?

- What can I do to deepen my focus on the task at hand?

- What strategies can I employ to stay focused when I am working online?

# Treating Yourself to a Midday Walk

Going outdoors is an important part of a mindfulness practice. If you start to fidget and feel restless during the day, a bit of fresh air and nature can do wonders. Whether you live by the water, in a city, in the suburbs, or in the country, fresh air can do so much for your focus, mind-set, and energy levels.

I do my midday mindful walk around the same time each day. I notice that a sense of dread comes over me around 1:00 p.m., and I start to have trouble completing tasks. I can sense that I need something that mindless tidying or task-switching cannot satisfy. So each day at a similar time, I put on my shoes and head out for a short mindful walk. My mind and body now crave this habit to get centered and redirect difficult thinking patterns to more positive ones.

You can plan to do this walk on a work break, between classes, or anytime you are able to get outside. When might be the best time for you to go for a mindful walk each day? Give it a try and notice how your mood and mind-set are uplifted.

1.  Go outside. Take a few deep breaths and decide on a short walk path.

2.  Set an intention to just walk. (Keep your phone out of your hands, don't wear headphones, don't listen to or talk to anyone on any device, and don't eat or drink anything.)

3.  As you walk at a pleasant pace, use your senses to observe the world around you. Take it in. What do you smell? What do you hear? What do you see? What do you feel on your skin?

4.  When you return from your walk, notice how you feel. How are your mood and energy level now? What has shifted for you?

# Practicing the Zoom Lens of Attention

🕐 TIME: 2–5 MINUTES

To focus your attention, it can be helpful to use your eyes like a zoom lens for the drishti gaze. A drishti is a point you look at to focus your eyes. This concentration tool can also improve balance. Starting with the drishti, zoom out, and zoom back in. The first part of this exercise should take about a minute. The second part may take two to four minutes.

## STEP-BY-STEP GUIDE FOR DRISHTI GAZE

1. Stand up and look straight ahead of you.

2. Find a fixed point (something not moving) in the distance and keep your eyes gently focused there.

3. Shift your weight and come to stand on one foot, keeping your eyes on the focal point.

4. Come back to center and shift your weight to the other side, coming to stand on the other foot, again keeping your eyes on the focal point.

5. Return to center and notice how you feel.

## STEP-BY-STEP GUIDE FOR THE ZOOM LENS OF ATTENTION

1. Stand tall and find your drishti gaze.

2. Zoom in so you are looking mainly at the focal point.

3. When you feel ready to expand your attention, start to intentionally take in more of the area in your periphery. Imagine zooming out with your eyes to take in the sides of the space you are in. Note how you feel. Could you see more when you focused on expanding your attention?

4. Just as you did to take in the periphery, take in the depths of the space you are in by also expanding your field of vision up and down.

5. Bring your attention back to the focal point and notice how you feel.

TIP: *Now that you have experienced the zoom lens of attention, try the same zooming in and out with your listening. What is that like?*

# Breathing with Joy

Do you ever feel tired and unmotivated, like you are dreading what you have to do next? This sensation tends to hit me in the afternoon between 2 and 5 p.m. To counteract this afternoon slump, I recommend the breath of joy activity—a fun, active, and quick mood-booster and pick-me-up. You will need enough space to stand up and reach your arms up and out to the sides. Enjoy this moment of joy in your beautiful life.

1. Stand up and shake out your arms and legs.

2. Find a nice, tall stance, letting your arms drop by your sides.

3. Extend both arms in front of you at hip height and inhale quickly and sharply through the nose. Don't exhale yet.

4. Inhale sharply again as you move your extended arms out to the sides. Don't exhale yet.

5. Inhale sharply one last time as you reach your arms up, elbows hugging toward your ears.

6. Exhale the sound "hah" as you drop your arms and let your belly fold toward your thighs with your head gently dropping down.

7. Repeat this sequence five times. Notice your energy and mood now.

# Noticing and Releasing Tension

⏲ TIME: 5–10 MINUTES

Pausing to notice and release tension throughout the day helps get your energy flowing again. Challenging emotions, hard physical work, mindless posture, and even simply existing can cause tension. Be gentle with yourself. Some tension is needed in the body for structural support, to literally hold you together. As you do this body scan, give yourself permission to retain some tension while releasing what you can. Whatever you can do now is perfect.

As you follow the instructions for the body scan, go as slowly as you want, taking 5 to 10 seconds (or more) for each body part. You may want to do your right side first and then the left, or both sides together. There is no one correct way to do the body scan. In mindfulness meditation, it starts in the toes; in yogic sleep (yoga nidra), it starts in the right-hand thumb. Here, we start in the head and move down to ground, calm, and simplify.

1. Take a mindful seat, and breathe in and out a few times (see "Taking a Mindful Seat," page 26).

2. Turn your focus inward. Place your hands in your lap, palms facing down.

3. Bring your awareness to the head—face, eyes, mouth, jaw, nose, and throat. Relax your muscles and release tension wherever you can. Note where you retain some tension without judging it.

4. Continue the body scan down into your throat, shoulders, upper back, chest, ribs, middle back, belly, lower back, arms, hands, and fingers. Continue to release tension.

5. Take your attention into the lower body, scanning the hips, pelvic region, glutes, thighs, knees, shins, calves, ankles, and feet. End the body scan in the bottom of both feet.

6. Note your entire body, checking for tension and relaxation. Give yourself one more opportunity to release the tension.

7. Thank yourself for taking time for this practice.

# Savoring the First Bite

⏱ TIME: 3–5 MINUTES

One of the classic exercises in the Mindfulness-Based Stress Reduction training course is to slowly, mindfully eat a raisin. In this activity, the instructor guides you through a 13-minute experience into your senses as you eat a single raisin. This activity is similar but shorter. Once you've had experience savoring your first bite, you can try this mindfulness activity when you sit down to eat lunch.

Choose a healthy food for this activity, such as a section of orange, a small square of chocolate, a blueberry, or a raisin. You will be using each of your senses to take in the food even before you eat it. You will slow down before your first bite (in ways you perhaps never have) to discover the joys of antici-pation, the sensations of your mouth and stomach preparing for nourishment, and the rich experience of being totally engrossed in your senses as you take a single bite. Don't be surprised if you notice a stronger, more delicious experience! Eating patterns tend to be hard to break, so if you scarf the first bite, simply rinse your mouth, slow down, and kindly allow yourself to try again.

1. Hold the food in your hand, and examine the visual details.

2. Sniff the food, then lick it. If it's fruit, break the cellulose cover to release the smells. Take in the scent for one minute.

3. Run your tongue through your mouth and note the taste before you eat.

4. Place the food on your tongue without chewing or swallowing. Leave it there for as long as you can to notice what happens in your mouth and stomach. Observe for 30 seconds.

5. Once you must chew, do so very slowly. Note the taste, sounds, sensations, and smells. Go intentionally slowly for about one minute.

6. When you must swallow, note where the sensation of the food in your mouth and throat vanishes into your stomach.

7. Take a moment to note how you feel, then write your observations in your journal.

# Sending a Note of Thanks

Gratitude is an antidote to stress. When you find yourself stressed during your day, pause for a moment to be with that feeling, then name it: "I am feeling stressed." If you decide you'd like to transform the feeling, choose someone in your life to thank.

## STEP-BY-STEP GUIDE

1. Sit comfortably with your eyes closed. Take a few deep breaths. Be with your strong emotion. Relax whatever tension you can. When you feel receptive to it, begin to ponder the prompt, "Who am I grateful for and why?"

2. See what comes up. You may need to scan your mind to think of people in your life for whom you are grateful. Or you may sit quietly and your gentle, open heart might help you feel the depth of love and appreciation for someone. There is no single way to go about this. Thinking and feeling are valid paths to gratitude. This step can take from one to five minutes or longer, so honor the pace you need.

3. Once you have the person in mind and feel how they have touched your life, breathe with that knowledge. Take two to three minutes to sit and ponder how that person has impacted you.

4. When you feel ready, write a sincere note of gratitude to that person. This message will warm your heart *and* theirs. If you're writing a paper note that must be mailed, I suggest doing the stamp, envelope, and mailing all at once so you don't lose the opportunity to complete the task. If you have chosen a deceased person, you can imagine them receiving this gratitude note.

5. Upon completing the task, note how you feel. Congratulations on completing this activity! ♡

# Reflecting with Reverence

A common belief in Western culture is the idea that in order to have value, we need to achieve goals. This notion can cause us to feel as though the goalposts are constantly moving ahead, no matter how much we do and how hard we work. If you have a tendency to move on to the next thing rather than first acknowledging your accomplishments (big and small), reflecting on them, and thanking yourself for your efforts, this activity is for you.

Whether you have completed a monumental goal such as graduating from a long-term program or a minor task like crossing something off your to-do list, savor the moment of completion with reverence and reflection. As you are approaching completion on an important-to-you task, acknowledge that you are on the verge of being done. For bigger things, like applying for and getting a promotion, the celebration is obvious because you will get an official offer. For graduations, book launches, and other time-specific goals, a date is approaching. Many of these major accomplishments include celebratory events.

In this activity, start with learning to celebrate yourself for smaller accomplishments, such as completing a tedious chore or doing a difficult part of your job. Sometimes the encouragement we most need comes from within.

1. Take a mindful seat (see "Taking a Mindful Seat," page 26). Note that you have accomplished something that was challenging in some way.

2. Reflect on all the steps, efforts, and growing you did to achieve this task. You can recall each step and experience in sequence or visualize the aspects of your journey, not necessarily in linear order. The time you spend on this step will vary based on the length of your journey.

3. Next, place one warm, heavy hand on your heart and close your eyes. Note and label your feelings and physical sensations as you study your inner experience, such as, "I notice warmth and joy. I notice discomfort and anxiety."

4. Bow your head in sincere gratitude to yourself. If this practice is new for you, it may be uncomfortable at first, and that's okay.

5. Sit quietly in reverence and observe your inner state. Breathe in and out, and when you're ready, consciously leave your mindful seat and move on with your day.

# Rewarding Yourself for Follow-Through

⏱ TIME: 1–2 MINUTES

Throughout any ordinary day, we must sometimes tackle jobs we would rather not do. When you take the time to mindfully reward yourself afterward, feel-good chemicals are released in your brain, the way they are when we get "likes" or comments on a social-media post.

This activity helps you relish in the delight of the chemical response in your brain from your very own attention. This experience is the definition of an intrinsic reward. In mindfulness, we seek to relinquish our grip on the need for constant external validation. This activity, when repeated regularly, can help you develop a positive inner voice that includes self-validation. All you need is a daily to-do list, a pen, and some follow-through.

1. To get in the flow, start with the easier or more enjoyable tasks on your to-do list.

2. When you cross off each task on your list, mindfully give yourself a "like" or positive comment.

3. Once you've crossed off a few things, you're likely ready to handle the task you've been dreading. For added motivation, you can keep your mind focused on the feeling you will get when you cross it off your list. However, avoid *talking* about your feelings of accomplishment with anyone until after you have finished the task to avoid tricking your brain into rewarding you prematurely, thereby ruining your motivation.

4. When you complete the dreaded task, grab your to-do list and cross it off. Note how amazing you feel and enjoy the sensation for a few mindful moments.

5. At the end of the day, make a list of the tasks you accomplished. If you like doing so, create a journal dedicated to celebrating your daily accomplishments.

# Moving in Your Chair

If you have a sedentary job or hobby, you may become so focused on what you are doing that you lose connection with your body. To become present to your physical needs, begin to notice when your back or hips need attention. Chair yoga can help you address your body's needs, connecting you to the present moment. The following stretches are meant to be done as a sequence, but you can choose among them if you are short on time.

### STEP-BY-STEP GUIDE FOR HIP STRETCH

1. Take a mindful seat in your work chair (see "Taking a Mindful Seat," page 26). Get up and sit back down if necessary. Remember to keep your spine straight and away from the back of the chair.

2. Place your right ankle over your left thigh. Flex your toes toward your right knee.

3. Sit up tall. Feel into your right hip. The sensation should come from the outer right hip and into the center of your right glute.

4. Slowly, with your spine lengthened, hinge forward at the hips. Note when you have enough stretch in your right hip (no pain, just tension), and stop there.

5. Take 5 to 10 breaths in this position. Release and repeat the sequence on the other side.

### STEP-BY-STEP GUIDE FOR SHOULDER OPENING

1. Sit up tall in your mindful seat with your feet grounded on the floor and your spine straight and away from the back of the chair.

2. Reach your right arm forward from your shoulder, with your palm open and turned in and your fingers stretched outward.

3. Keeping your arm straight, slowly raise it until your arm hugs your right ear.

4. Bend your elbow and let your hand tap toward the center of your upper back, extending the elbow up toward the ceiling (you will feel this stretch in your right tricep). Simultaneously, press your neck into your right hand/arm to keep your neck from protruding forward.

5. Take 5 to 10 breaths in this position. Release and repeat the sequence on the other side.

*continues* ▶

## STEP-BY-STEP GUIDE FOR CHEST
## AND SHOULDER OPENING

1. Sit up tall in your mindful seat, and lift up tall through your chest as you simultaneously root down through your seat.

2. Extend your arms wide with your elbows bent at a 90-degree angle.

3. Draw your elbows behind you, squeezing your shoulder blades toward the center of your back. Take five breaths.

4. Bring your arms forward in a hugging motion, allowing your elbows to cross at the center at the height of your shoulders with your right elbow on top. As you hug yourself, try to bring your fingertips around your back on each side, grabbing for your shoulder blades if you can reach. Take five breaths into your upper back.

5. Repeat the steps, ending with your left arm on top, and take five breaths into your upper back.

6. Note how your body feels for a few mindful moments, then return to your task.

# Awakening Your Energy

If you are in the midst of a midday slump and find your-self reaching for caffeine or longing to take a nap, spend 10 mindful minutes on this active yoga flow instead. Doing this sequence many awaken your energy so you can forgo sleep or another cup of coffee or tea.

If you are frequently exhausted during the day, you may need to sleep better at night. Try some of the mind-fulness activities in the next chapter to prepare yourself for better sleep. For now, I invite you now to try some active, powerful, invigorating yoga postures. Do this sequence on a yoga mat, carpet, or towel. Breathe deeply, quietly, and steadily throughout.

## STEP-BY-STEP GUIDE

1. Mountain pose to warrior 1 pose: Stand tall with arms by your sides. Root through your feet as you lift your heart and the crown of your head toward the ceiling. Lengthen upward and downward actively. Step your right leg back. With hands on your hips, steer your hip points to the front of the mat. Make both legs strong and bend your left knee over your ankle. As you do, lift from your waist and make your spine tall and strong.

Raise your extended arms up, palms facing in, elbows by your ears. Breathe five times, then step your right foot forward and repeat on the left side.

2. Chair pose: Stand up tall. Bring your big toes to touch with your heels slightly apart. With hands on your knees, start to sit your hips back and down, placing the weight in your heels. Sit as low as you can while keeping your core strong and maintaining your spine's natural curve. Press your hands into your knees to raise and broaden your chest. If your spine feels okay, raise your arms to shoulder height with your palms facing in. Take 5 to 10 breaths, observing sensations and temperature.

3. Warrior 2 pose: Stand up tall. Step your feet apart wider than your shoulders, or about three feet apart. Turn your right foot out to the right and bend your right knee over your ankle. Keep your spine tall over your pelvis as you actively open your hips and chest to the side. Extend your arms at the shoulders to the sides, roll your shoulders back, and reach long through your hands and fingers. Turn your head to look over your right middle finger and beyond. Take 10 breaths and then repeat on the other side. Notice your energetic state.

# Becoming What You Think

The Buddha is quoted as saying, "The mind is everything. What you think you become." The reality taking place in our minds can shape how we see ourselves and the world. It can make the experience we live one of beauty or suffering. Pain and change are parts of life, but suffering takes place in the mind. Many meditation teachers say that suffering is a choice. You have the choice to shape your mind using positive affirmations, which can influence how you see yourself.

Don't worry if you do lots of negative thinking. Our brains are hardwired to protect us from danger. Humans have a built-in negativity bias, and we see patterns and assume danger is coming even when it isn't. This tendency can backfire, however, when we try to stop merely surviving and start thriving.

This negativity bias benefited our ancestors, but it can really hold us back. Negative thoughts about ourselves can be triggered by circumstances that remind us of past stressors or when something new is afoot. Here's an example from my life: When things are changing around me or change is on the horizon, I hear lots of negative thoughts about my ability to adapt. My negative belief around having a lack of resilience caused so much anxiety that it robbed me of energy, attention, and joy. To counteract this habit, I came up with a mantra: "I adapt to the changes in my life with steadiness and grace." You can also develop a mantra to counteract negative self-talk.

STEP–BY–STEP GUIDE

1. Next time you feel a lack of confidence or hear your negative self-talk (in your head or through self-deprecating comments spoken aloud), grab a pen and your journal and go somewhere you can be alone for 10 minutes.

2. Lie down if you can and take a few deep breaths, then get ready to write.

3. Write about the belief you have about yourself that is robbing you of your energy, attention, and joy. How would your life benefit from a new worldview? Create a mantra to counteract this belief and write it down.

4. Set an intention to study your mind and begin to notice when you start to pick on yourself. State your mantra when you notice these negative thoughts.

# Wishing You Well

During the day, people are bound to frustrate or irritate you. If you are losing your cool, remember that all people just want to be happy, healthy, and at peace. Instead of venting or gossiping, wish the other person well with this loving-kindness meditation. I know it may sound like woo-woo, but wishing others well when they have wronged or bothered you is freeing. A 2013 study published in *Psychological Science* has shown that practicing the loving-kindness meditation regularly increases compassion. It can help you replace feelings of anger with those of love and kindness.

1. Picture someone who is easy to love. This person should not be the individual who bothered you, but rather a friend you have had little contention with, a child, or even a pet. Visualize that person's face. Mentally or aloud repeat three times:

   💬 *"May you be happy.*
   *May you be healthy.*
   *May you feel peace.*
   *May you be released from suffering."*

2. Once you have the hang of sending loving-kindness to someone easy, try doing this meditation for the person who hurt you. Visualize their face. Mentally or aloud repeat three times:

   💬 *"May you be happy.*
   *May you be healthy.*
   *May you feel peace.*
   *May you be released from suffering."*

# Writing Down Your Challenges

You are going about your day, and everything is running smoothly. Suddenly, you get stuck and can't move forward because you are unsure, distracted, discouraged, or feeling some other block. Spend a few mindful minutes journaling to get to the root of your challenge and come up with a positive affirmation to help you through.

Respond to these journal prompts:

> Which task(s) am I stuck on?

> What about this task(s) do I dread or prefer to avoid?

> What strategies might help me manage tackling this task(s)?

> Is it possible for me to break down my task(s) into smaller tasks? What mini or micro tasks can help me manage this task(s)?

> Do I need to warm up to this more challenging task by first completing ones I enjoy, or would I benefit from doing this harder task first? What might work best for me?

> What positive affirmation/mantra can I repeat to myself to help me overcome this aversion? Some examples include "I can do hard things," "Even though it's hard, I will follow through," "When I complete my *(fill in the blank)*, I will reward myself with *(fill in the blank)*," and "I can handle anything."

After you have completed your journal entry and have created a mantra, take a mindful seat (see "Taking a Mindful Seat," page 26). Repeat your manta silently or aloud 5 to 10 times. Conjure the feeling of gratitude as though your intention has already come true. Now get back to work! You got this! You can use this mantra the next time you feel stuck, too.

# Self-Compassion Booster

Many of us have challenges with self-confidence and self-love, manifested through negative self-talk, self-deprecating language, feelings of unworthiness, or the dreaded impostor syndrome (a pattern of thinking in which an individual doubts their ability and fears that others see them as a fraud).

The more you practice mindfulness, the more you will come to understand that you are whole, perfect, and complete right now. You do not need to change a single aspect of yourself to be worthy of love, admiration, and care. When you start to manifest feelings of self-love, you can more skillfully, blissfully, and presently tackle the world one breath at a time and grow in confidence.

Doesn't knowing you are whole and perfect right now make you feel more peaceful about this journey of self-transformation? Even if you know you are destined to take flight like a butterfly, embrace the caterpillar you are today. If you are the butterfly, know that your current form will pass away as part of the natural cycle of life. You will need to blossom again from some kind of seed throughout life's many transitions. You can embrace all forms of yourself as whole, perfect, and complete every step of the way.

This activity is the most challenging in the chapter, and it can make you highly emotional. Attempt it only on days when you are feeling stable. If you are experiencing emotional upheaval, wait until you have attained a more balanced state. Thank you for heeding my advice.

STEP-BY-STEP GUIDE

1. Take a mindful seat in front of a mirror (see "Taking a Mindful Seat," page 26). Take a breath or two to get centered, then close your eyes.

2. What negative statement were you making about yourself? Go inward and note the hurt that is there.

3. Take a moment to be with the hurt. Do not skip over it or pretend it isn't there. Feel and observe it.

4. Imagine giving the hurt part of you a big hug. Nurture your hurt and let it know you are here to care for it. Mentally say to yourself, "I love you. I am here."

5. Now that you feel your own presence and commitment, open your eyes. Look into your eyes. Do not close them or look away.

6. Repeat the following 10 times: "I love you. I'm sorry. Please forgive me. Thank you."

7. Once you complete the 10 repetitions, take a moment to place a warm, heavy hand on your heart and bring awareness to your emotional state.

# MINDFUL NIGHTS

When you picture your perfect evening, how does it look, feel, and sound? Now think about how you tend to spend your nights. Many of us have little separation between our daily work, chores, or studies and our evenings. Some of us let the light from our devices keep our minds alert until we pass out, disturbing what could have been a truly restful sleep.

Imagine another way: You take time to consciously close out your workday. You dim the lights and play soothing sounds to make your home peaceful and calming. You change your clothing into something more comfortable, a tactile and visual reminder that you are shifting down. You fully power down your devices or at least put them on silent. You step outside the hamster wheel of automaticity and turn instead to deeply soothing mindfulness practices that prepare your mind and body for a nourishing, restful night. I invite you to do so now. Come on in.

# Closing Out the Day Ritual

What marks the shift from your busy day to your night? Is it the setting sun? If you happen to work the typical Western 9-to-5 shift, perhaps 5 p.m. is your marker. If you are a parent, your marker might be when your child's homework is done. If you do not have a traditional schedule, you may not have clear markers. Do you know what makes your official work time come to an end? If you don't have a marker, chances are you need a firmer boundary between your working hours and your time for rest. You can transform your nights with a little practice, discipline, awareness, and compassion.

## STEP-BY-STEP GUIDE

1. Choose a time that is reasonable to stop the busyness of the day. When you have determined it's time to wind down, go to your sanctuary and take a mindful seat (see "Taking a Mindful Seat," page 26).

2. Go into your mind and review your day, recalling all that stands out about your morning and afternoon. Sit with each memory and take a complete breath in and out for each. Hold space in appreciation for all that took place.

3. After spending a few minutes recapping and honoring your day, acknowledge that you are mindfully entering into the night. Visualize how you'd like your night to go. Make a mental note of the things you still need to do to get into a fully restful place (for example, feed the kids and get them ready for bed, change into cozy clothes, etc.).

4. Take a few breaths with your plan in mind. Note any feeling of dread or urgency that may result from having more to do. Allow any feelings that may arise, greeting them with a mental "Hello, it's nice to see you again." Refrain from resisting any emotions. Once you greet your feelings, nurture the part of you that is challenged, mentally stating, "I am here for you."

5. Mindfully, with calm, go about transforming yourself and your space for the evening. Dim the lights, put on calming music, wash your face, and turn off devices.

TIP: *If you decide to turn off devices to close out your day, you might initially feel some anxiety. It will get easier: According to Myla and Jon Kabat-Zinn's book,* Everyday Blessings: The Inner Work of Mindful Parenting, *the difficulty of removing technology from a habituated practice lasts only about two weeks.*

# Spending Time in Your Sanctuary

Regardless of whether you've used your sanctuary as a space for closing out the day, visit the space at some point during the evening to venture inward. How will you know when it's time to turn inward? Notice when you are mindlessly scrolling through your phone or TV channels, or searching the refrigerator or pantry when you're not hungry. If you are restless, it's the perfect time for a visit.

## STEP-BY-STEP GUIDE

1.  Go to your sanctuary. Arrange any objects as you wish. Perk up your sense of smell with an essential oil mist or incense, if desired.

2.  Take a mindful seat, facing your sanctuary or altar (see "Taking a Mindful Seat," page 26). Look at the objects you placed in your sanctuary. Notice their physical appearance.

3.  Close your eyes and bring that same level of noticing and attention to your inward experience.

4. Keeping your eyes closed and relaxed, draw your inner gaze to either the third-eye center (which resides between and just above your eyebrows) or the heart center (which resides in the center of your chest). Bring your inner gaze there by gently directing the energy of your eyes to the spot that feels more energetic or active. Do not strain your eyes.

5. Breathe, keeping your inward gaze in your chosen spot, or returning it there if your inner gaze wanders. Notice what thoughts, sensations, and emotions are present without judging them as right or wrong.

6. Continue breathing for the remainder of time or until you feel your energy settle.

TIP: *If neither spot stands out in step four, simply choose one. I usually go with my heart if I am trying to feel aligned with my emotions and my third eye if I'd like to feel in tune with my intuition.*

# Putting Your Feet Up

When you need to rest but aren't quite ready for bed, try this inversion yoga pose. All you need is a couch or a wall, with a rug or yoga mat for your back. This gentle relaxation posture helps improve circulation, reduce swelling in the feet and legs, and restore tired feet.

## STEP-BY-STEP GUIDE

1. Sit with your right hip against the wall or couch. Lie down, swinging your legs up the couch or wall. If your hamstrings are tight, wiggle away a little bit to change the hip angle from 90 degrees or the shape of an L to an obtuse angle, slightly wider than 90 degrees.

2. If you are using a wall, your legs will be more or less straight. With the couch, your legs will be bent at the knees. In both cases, the legs should be heavy, resting on the support of the wall or couch.

3. Let the floor and wall or couch hold your weight, allowing yourself to relax deeper and deeper into your supports.

4. Place your hands on your belly, palms facing down, or let your arms rest beside you, palms facing up, depending on which position feels best.

5. Close your eyes, and breathe deeply and steadily. Spend 5 to 10 minutes relaxing in this position. Stay longer if you feel like it.

# Preparing a Healthy Snack with Full Attention

🕐 TIME: 5 MINUTES

Do you find yourself getting distracted by your devices even when you're doing something quick and easy, like preparing an early evening snack? If you have trouble staying on task, practice giving your full attention to preparing a healthy snack, such as fruit or vegetables. With practice, you can bring your full mindful attention to other activities as well.

## STEP-BY-STEP GUIDE

1. As you choose your snack, feel the temperature and notice the color, weight, and other features of the food.

2. Take a moment to consider where this food was grown. What was required to get it to you? Be mindful of the time it took to grow (for example, some trees take years to bear fruit). Consider the people and machines involved in picking, storing, shipping, and selling you the food.

3. Rinse the produce. Take your time peeling or cutting it into neat pieces. Create a pleasant arrangement on a dish.

4. Take a mindful seat (see "Taking a Mindful Seat," page 26). Recall the activity on page 66, when you savored your first bite.

5. Mindfully enjoy the flavors, sensations, and gratitude you have for acknowledging the journey involved in getting your food to you.

# Soothing Moon Flow

⏱ TIME: 10 MINUTES

This relaxing sequence from crescent moon to frog squat to ragdoll is a slow moving meditation to mindfully prepare your body for the lunar energy of sleep. Do this activity on a yoga mat, carpet, or towel.

### STEP-BY-STEP GUIDE

1. Crescent moon: Stand up tall, reaching your arms to the sky. Interlace your fingers and stretch tall. As you inhale, ground into your feet. Squeeze your arms by your ears. As you exhale, arch to the left, feeling a stretch in the right side of your rib cage. Keep your hips and chest facing the front. (Your hips and shoulders may want to twist, so you might want to practice in front of a mirror at first.) Breathe for 5 to 10 breath cycles. Come back to center for a breath, lengthen again, and repeat the crescent moon on the left side.

2. Frog squat: Step your feet mat-distance apart and allow your toes to point out on both sides. Slowly start to squat down like a frog by bending your knees deeply and allowing them to open to each side. If you are flexible, avoid flopping down into this pose by remaining

active in your glutes and pressing firmly through your feet. If you are less flexible and this pose is not comfortable, don't force yourself down any farther than your body is ready for. In your frog squat, press your palms firmly together at your heart center as you nudge your knees open with your elbows. Lift your heart tall and tuck your chin slightly. Take 5 to 10 breaths. Stand up carefully.

3. Ragdoll pose: Prepare to fold forward. With your hands on your hips, slowly fold your head down toward the floor, keeping your knees bent enough that your belly touches or almost touches your thighs. Release your head down. Point your toes forward, feet slightly apart. Grab your opposite elbows and hang in ragdoll pose. Take 5 to 10 breaths. Slowly come back to your standing position.

# Feeling Your Cozy Clothes

⏱ TIME: 2–3 MINUTES

To mark the end of the workday, it's nice to put on something comfortable for an enjoyable sensory experience. As you change your clothing, make it a mindful experience.

## STEP-BY-STEP GUIDE

1. Select your pajamas, dim the lights, and get ready to shift your energy.

2. Remove your clothing from the day, being mindful of the work you did, the challenges you overcame, and the tasks you accomplished.

3. Place your day clothing in the laundry basket to keep your space tidy. Hang up or fold any items that don't have to be washed. Allow this process to help you separate the time for doing from the time for being.

4. Put on your comfortable clothing. Notice how it feels and fits.

5. Close your eyes while standing or sitting in a mindful seat (see "Taking a Mindful Seat," page 26). Notice the sensation of the fabric on your skin. Notice where the clothing makes contact with your skin and where it does not. Spend some time focusing on the sensation of the clothing. Feel for texture, weight, fit, and fabric. How much can you become aware of as you observe your sensations for two to three minutes?

6. Take a few deep breaths and continue with your evening.

# Turning Down the Lights

Dimming the lights is good way to shift the energy from doing to being, from day to night. During the day, we need the bright light and open curtains to awaken our minds so we can accomplish our important tasks. At night, we need to let our minds and bodies know it's time to power down.

## STEP-BY-STEP GUIDE

1. Whether you have dimmer switches, electric candles, wax candles, or some other way to change your lighting from active to relaxing, shift the energy of the space to darker, calmer, softer lighting.

2. Note how your eyes can relax more as you dim the lighting. Turn off all bright screens if you can, including phones, televisions, and monitors. Let your eyes be removed from excess lighting.

3.  You may choose to close your blinds to remove any lighting from outside, especially if you live in a city or near any homes with bright lights.

4.  Take a few minutes to acclimate your eyes to the new lighting. Sit up tall in a mindful seat (see "Taking a Mindful Seat," page 26) and allow your eyes to be slightly open. Breathe deeply, gently, and slowly, pausing at the top of the inhale and exhale.

5.  Note how you feel after two to three minutes of dimmer lighting. Enjoy.

# Observing the Surrounding Sounds

🕐 TIME: 5 MINUTES

One of the beautiful things about nighttime is the changing soundscape. In the morning, we listen for birds and the sounds of the bustling, energy-bursting time of sunrise. In the evening, we can listen to the world quiet down. There is something quite interesting about tapping in to the sounds of the nighttime from a quiet, openhearted place. You can do this activity inside or outside, but if you live in an area that comes alive at night, do it indoors.

## STEP-BY-STEP GUIDE

1. Take a mindful seat on a cushion, chair, or park bench (see "Taking a Mindful Seat," page 26). You may need a blanket to stay warm. Set your timer for five minutes.

2. Close your eyes and turn inward. Tune in to your sense of hearing. You might even imagine your ears perking up.

3. What sounds may indicate night has fallen? Listen to the sounds all around you, and notice where they are originating. Listen to the sounds as long as they are happening and notice when or if they cease. Play with listening to sounds nearby and far away, high and low, outside and inside you.

4. Once your timer chimes, take a moment to notice how you feel. Perhaps jot down the effects of your practice in your journal, then mindfully return to your evening.

# Anchoring Your Mind

Imagine it's the end of your day and you want to relax, but you can't stop thinking about something. Rumination is a part of life, but it's not productive, especially at night, because it can lead to sleepless nights and worry. Anchoring your thoughts is one way to bring your mind back to focus, even if it wanders endlessly. Your only job is to notice that your mind has wandered and bring it back with kindness and curiosity.

Picture a heavy anchor in the ocean chained to a boat. Imagine waves buoying the boat. Your mind is the boat. Your thoughts are the waves that can carry the boat away. The anchor is your breath. The anchor prevents the boat from sailing off. Although the anchor holds the boat nearby, it does not prevent the boat from moving around. In this meditation, you will use your breath as the anchor to bring your mind back—but, like a boat, expect your mind to move about. Use awareness of breath to anchor it.

The first time you do this activity, set a timer for 3 minutes. With more experience, work toward 10 minutes.

1. Take a mindful seat in your sanctuary (see "Taking a Mindful Seat," page 26). Breathe in and out a few times to get your body settled. Close your eyes and turn inward.

2. Release any breathing technique and simply observe your breath as it comes in and out of your nose, as it fills and empties your belly.

3. As you sit, notice when you are thinking and mentally state, "Thinking."

4. As soon as you label a thought, bring your attention back to noticing your natural breath. Do not apply judgment around thoughts appearing. If you judge yourself and get disappointed or angry, remind yourself that thoughts are a natural product of a healthy brain. Simply use kindness to redirect your focus to the breath.

5. After your timer goes off, take a moment to notice the quality of your thoughts and attention. Notice how your mind is experiencing the present moment.

# Letting Your
# Thoughts Flow

🕐 TIME: 5–10 MINUTES

If you find yourself endlessly thinking about something that happened during the day, try to process it through stream-of-consciousness journaling. Write without the goal of making your writing perfect or beautiful. Simply get your thoughts out on paper and find a way to write back to gratitude. No matter how stressful, challenging, perplexing, or mysterious your topic, see if you can circle back to gratitude by the end of your journal entry. Before you close your journal, consider how you can find an opportunity for growth and gratitude in your writing. Finish by taking a few deep breaths. Feel free to read what you've written or follow up with "Anchoring Your Mind" on page 106.

TIP: *If you don't like writing by hand, consider using a traditional typewriter so you don't have to turn on your computer, which is a source of distraction. If you have trouble writing open-ended entries, make a list or create a structure to your writing such as: (1) define the thought, (2) write your feelings about it, (3) write what you know to be true about it, and (4) bring your mind to gratitude.*

*Wynken, Blynken, and Nod one night*
*Sailed off in a wooden shoe,—*
*Sailed on a river of crystal light*
*Into a sea of dew.*
*"Where are you going, and what do you wish?"*
*The old moon asked the three.*
*"We have come to fish for the herring-fish*
*That live in this beautiful sea;*
*Nets of silver and gold have we,"*
*Said Wynken,*
*Blynken,*
*And Nod.*

—Excerpt from "Wynken, Blynken, and Nod"
by Eugene Field

# Breathing into Your Belly and Heart

⏱ TIME: 2–5 MINUTES

Anytime you need to slow down, give yourself some warmth and compassion and just breathe. This exercise is a great bedtime breath, and it also works well after you put the kids to sleep, when you have a conflict with someone, or if you just need to soothe. I love it at nighttime, but it's perfect all day. It's important to inhale through your nose, but you can exhale through your nose or mouth—whatever is comfortable.

STEP-BY-STEP GUIDE

1. Take a mindful seat or lie down (see "Taking a Mindful Seat," page 26). Get comfortable.

2. Place a warm, heavy hand on your heart and a warm, heavy hand on your belly. Notice the warmth of your hands.

3. Take long, slow breaths in through your nose. Allow your belly to fill. As you breathe out, empty your belly and pull your navel gently toward your spine.

4. With your subsequent breaths, slowly bring the breath above your belly into your ribs and eventually your chest. Expand the breath upward slowly. Take three to four breaths or more into your belly before you inflate your ribs. Take three to four breaths into your ribs before you expand your breath as high as your chest and collarbones. (If you can't get the breath to rise into your chest from your belly, don't worry. With repetition and practice, you will be able to take larger breaths.)

5. Release the breath as slowly as you can through your nose, without feeling stressed out.

6. Complete 10 to 15 breath cycles. Observe your state of being and notice how you feel.

# Appreciate Slowing Down

🕐 TIME: 10 MINUTES

Mahatma Gandhi is quoted as saying, "There is more to life than increasing speed." To drop deeply into true relaxation, you need to consciously slow down. The contemporary culture seems to beg us to do more in each 24-hour span than the day before. Mindfulness puts the emphasis on being. Being means doing less, slowing down, and tapping into the beauty that is the intentionality in moving into stillness.

## STEP-BY-STEP GUIDE

1. Take a little walk around your living quarters. Consciously move slowly. After a lap or two, lie on your back—perhaps on a yoga mat, rug, or blanket.

2. Bend your knees deeply and let your knees sway from side to side several times, allowing your neck and hips to move instinctively until you return to lying flat on your back.

3. Extend your legs and let your feet flop out. Let your arms rest, either bringing your hands on top of your heart or belly (or both) or letting them come to the floor.

4. As slowly as you can, breathe in and out. On each exhale, count back from 10 until you get to 1. If you lose track, start again at 10. As you count, slow down the breath as much as you can.

5. Release the breathing technique when you get to one or when you feel complete. You might want to repeat the counting several times until you feel settled.

6. Use your awareness to look for areas of tension you can release to relax more deeply. You may want to do the body scan you learned on page 65.

7. Remain lying down for as long as you wish. When you are done (you can set a 10-minute timer, if you wish), mindfully stand up. Notice how you feel.

# Channeling Your Energy Centers

This seated meditation takes your awareness through your energy centers, called chakras. Picture your body lengthwise from the crown of your head to the base of your spine at your tailbone. Imagine a hollow tube, inside which energy flows. When you posture yourself properly, that energy can flow with ease. Mindfully focus on where your energy is flowing with ease and where it may be stuck.

Visualize the hollow tube again, now with a colored sphere or orb at each of the following points:

> Red at the base of your spine

> Orange at your lower belly

> Yellow at your solar plexus (between your belly button and heart)

> Green at your heart center

> Blue at your throat

> Indigo at your third eye (just above your brow center)

> Golden at the crown of your head

These points are your seven chakras. This meditation takes you from the bottom chakra to the top, spending about 10 breaths (1 minute) at each one. Keep an attitude of intentional detachment about what this experience should feel like, and instead simply observe the sensation of energy flow or stagnation at each chakra. Keep your inward focus on each chakra as you breathe and observe without attachment to any particular outcome.

STEP-BY-STEP GUIDE

1.  Sitting up tall in your mindful seat (see "Taking a Mindful Seat," page 26), close your eyes and bring your attention to the bottom chakra at the base of your spine. Take a breath in and out, scanning this area. Visualize the red sphere and note if you feel energy flowing here. Mentally repeat, "I am safe and secure."

2.  Focus on the chakra at your lower belly, imagining an orange sphere around your navel. Mentally repeat, "I am creative," and note your energy.

3.  Move your awareness into the solar plexus, visualizing a yellow orb. Mentally repeat, "I am powerful," as you notice your energy flowing or stagnating here.

4.  Move your awareness into the center of your chest, picturing a spinning green orb. Mentally repeat, "I am love," and scan for the energetic flow.

    *continues* ▶

## ▶ Channeling Your Energy Centers
(continued)

5. Draw your attention into your throat, picturing a spinning blue orb. Mentally repeat, "I communicate with ease," as you scan for flow or stagnation.

6. Draw your awareness to the third-eye center, visualizing a spinning indigo sphere. Mentally repeat, "I follow my intuition," as you scan for the energetic flow.

7. Drawing your attention up to the crown of your head, picture a thousand-petaled lotus and a golden orb spinning from the crown of your head and above into the universe. Mentally repeat, "I am connected to all that is," as you scan for the energetic flow.

8. Imagine moving your energy up and down the central channel of your body, noting areas that feel more active and stagnant.

TIP: *From the areas of energetic flow and stagnation, you can draw wisdom for your life. Do not judge areas that aren't flowing as good or bad. Sometimes we need to protect our energy. We can wake up our dormant energy with dedication to practice, readiness, and discernment.*

# Balancing Your Breath

TIME: 5 MINUTES

In this breathing exercise, you'll practice a beginner's version of alternate nostril breathing by visualizing the air traveling through one nostril at a time rather than closing off alternate nostrils with your fingers. Before you start, check how much airflow each nostril has by pressing the other nostril closed with a finger and breathing in and out. It's normal for one nostril to be dominant at a time.

It's nice to have both nostrils open before you go to sleep to promote optimal health, so this is a great nighttime activity. Traditional alternate nostril breathing is known for balancing the right and left hemispheres of the brain. It allows the repair work to happen in your cells as well as the heating processes (such as digestion) to take place in your intestines. When you are new to this style of breathing, it may be difficult to get your breath to go through one nostril at a time. For now, just visualize the breath along with your hand movements as described.

1. Sit up tall in a mindful seat (see "Taking a Mindful Seat," page 26). Take a few regular breaths.

2. Open your left palm and make a fist with your right hand. Breathe in, visualizing the breath entering through your left nostril.

3. Make a fist with your left hand and open your right palm. Breathe out, visualizing the breath exiting through your right nostril.

4. With your right palm still open, visualize breathing in through the right nostril.

5. Now make a fist with your right hand, and open your left palm. Visualize breathing out through the left nostril.

6. Repeat steps 2 through 5 for 10 to 20 repetitions. Once you feel complete, notice how your mind and body feel.

TIP: *If you feel light-headed while doing this practice, take a break for a few moments.*

# Turning Inward: A Heart-Centered Meditation

⏲ TIME: 10 MINUTES

For this meditation, you will focus specifically on the energy in your heart center, or heart chakra. Instead of focusing on what's outside of you as you did for much of the day, you will tune in to your heart by turning your attention inward. Your inner gaze will be on your heart center throughout the meditation.

STEP-BY-STEP GUIDE

1. Using the utmost gentle inward gaze on your heart chakra, sit or lie down mindfully. If you are very tired, sit up to avoid falling asleep. If you are sure you can stay awake, lie down. Alternatively, prop up your legs on the wall or the couch, as you did in the "Putting Your Feet Up" activity on page 94.

2. Once you are in position, get settled and comfortable. Start by taking a few big breaths in through your nose and letting out audible sighs through your mouth. You may note some emotional release. You may also feel tension dissipate.

3. Draw your inner gaze to your heart. Stay there and feel the flow of energy in your heart. Do any images come to mind? Do any faces appear? Do you think of anyone or anything?

4. Once you have an image, a thought, or a person in your inner gaze, breathe gently for three to four breath cycles, keeping the image, thought, or person in the front of your mind. What are you feeling and learning by keeping your attention on this image, thought, or person? Is there some action you may decide to take as a result? Based on who or what is in your heart, what conclusions can you make about what's important to you?

5. After 10 minutes, come to a seated position if you've been lying down. If you have an additional 5 minutes, grab your journal to jot down your thoughts. What has the wisdom in your heart shown you?

# Loving-Kindness Meditation for Yourself

⏱ TIME: 3–5 MINUTES

Letting go of your day and moving into rest may take a tremendous amount of compassion for yourself. Why? Because if you're like many of the people of I've taught and coached, you may not feel like you've done enough to deserve to let go of work, worry, or emotional burdens at night. You do deserve the utmost care from yourself. No matter what you can accomplish, no matter what your employment or economic status, and no matter where you live, you deserve to feel happy, healthy, peaceful, and free—every single day.

Loving-kindness meditation has been shown in studies, including a 2013 study published in *Psychological Science*, to help increase feelings of compassion and empathy. In this meditation, you will direct love toward yourself. You did a variation of this for others in the "Wishing You Well" activity on page 82, but we saved the best for last. Wishing yourself well is a key skill in mindfulness practice.

1. Find a comfortable position, sitting or lying down. Place a warm, heavy hand on your heart and the other hand on top of it.

2. Bring your own image to your mind's eye. Picture yourself; see your face and body. With compassion in your heart, repeat the following out loud or mentally at least three times.

   *"May I be happy.*
   *May I be healthy.*
   *May I feel peace.*
   *May I be released from suffering."*

# Relaxing into Stillness

If pent-up energy is keeping you from winding down, prepare for this activity by mindfully noticing the energy that needs to be released. Choose a method to release it, such as push-ups, jumping jacks, a one-minute plank, or some other physical exertion. My preference is usually a few challenging yoga poses, but do what you like. After a few minutes, release the exercise by slowing down and then stopping. Now begin.

## STEP-BY-STEP GUIDE

1. On a yoga mat, towel, or carpet, get into child's pose by coming to your hands and knees, then pressing your butt toward your heels; walk your hands forward and bring your head down.

2. Stay in that position, gently rubbing your forehead into the mat, towel, or carpet as if you were giving it a massage, for 10 breaths.

3. Slowly flip onto your back. Lie flat with your arms at your sides and legs relaxed (corpse pose or savasana). Let go of all doing. A corpse doesn't do anything; it just is.

4. Invoke the energy of complete release. Do not control your breathing. Do not control your mind. Lie here for 3 to 5 minutes, slowly working your way up to 10 minutes over time. Feel free to use a timer, or simply lie there for as long as it feels good.

# Letting Go

This practice is detachment from the day. Grab your journal and pen. Take a moment to consider all the things you did today. Help yourself savor the accomplishments, credit yourself, and let all these things go. You do not need to keep thinking during a designated time of rest. Let your night be a mindfully restful time of detachment from working. Release yourself from the grips of mental work as much as you can.

This journaling activity not only allows you to celebrate all your hard work but also can help you put up healthy boundaries around thinking or talking about work-related things at night.

In your journal, make a list of all the day's accomplishments. Nothing is too small to make the list. Don't write about things you did not accomplish. (You can do that in another journal if you'd like, but it does not belong here.)

Once you've made your list, repeat this mantra three times: "I see my efforts and reflect love back to myself. I can rest. I can let go."

Write a list of people and things you are grateful for. List as many as you possibly can, even people you may have included previously. Now repeat this mantra three times:

💬 *"The world is abundant. I am grateful.*
*I am satiated. I have everything I need."*

# CONCLUSION

Congratulations on working your way through this book on mindfulness activities you can do in the morning, day, and evening. Whether you tried all of them or found some that resonated, you deserve a moment to bask in your hard work. You learned breathing techniques, meditations, movement practices, journaling, and focusing activities to support you in living a peaceful, present, and mindful life.

Choose some activities to practice daily and add them to your repertoire. Doing a little bit each day is key. Open this book again when you feel yourself go back on autopilot. Daily practice is the discipline needed to stoke your inner fire. That inner fire can burn bright the more fervently you practice. You do not need to achieve anything with your practice; simply showing up with your attention, awareness, and love is all I ask for you.

If you are called to, keep on going with your mindfulness and yoga practices. There are amazing teachers, books, workshops, trainings, and retreats that will continue to help you mold your life. Stay awake, compassionate, and present as you dive deeper. I am proud of you! Take a breath.

# RESOURCES

## RECOMMENDED AUTHORS

Peter Levine, Ph.D., has many books on healing trauma mindfully. If you suspect you have trauma, his books along with psychotherapy and a daily practice can really help.

Dan Siegel, author of many books for adults and children that use data and mindfulness to bring about personal transformation, is a must-read author.

## RECOMMENDED READING

*Everyday Blessings: The Inner Work of Mindful Parenting* by Myla and Jon Kabat-Zinn—A book on applying mindfulness to parenting

*Do Your Om Thing: Bending Yoga Tradition to Fit Your Modern Life* by Rebecca Pacheco—A book to learn the fundamentals of yoga philosophy

# RECOMMENDED WEBSITES

Flow and Grow Kids Yoga (FlowandGrowKidsYoga.com)—
Online yoga and mindfulness teacher trainings. If you want
to have a more mindful life with the children you love or
work with, join me in deepening your practice and making it
accessible to them. The shop includes curricula for yoga and
mindfulness.

Mindful (Mindful.org)—An amazing organization putting out
content on mindfulness that is ideal for beginners and inter-
mediates. They also offer trainings.

Mindfulness Beginners Book (MindfulnessBeginnersBook
.com)—This landing page for this book also includes bonus
videos and freebies.

Mindful Schools (MindfulSchools.org)—This organization
trains educators to bring mindfulness into schools.

Tara Brach (TaraBrach.com)—Tara is a psychologist and
mindfulness teacher who gives incredible dharma talks and
leads meditations. She is based in Maryland, and her meditations are available worldwide.

# REFERENCES

Brach, Tara. "Meditation: Gladdening the Mind." TaraBrach
.com, June 15, 2016. Audio recording, 18:05. tarabrach
.com/meditation-gladdening-mind/.

Kabat-Zinn, Myla, and Jon Kabat-Zinn. *Everyday Blessings:
The Inner Work of Mindful Parenting.* New York and
Boston: Hachette Books, 2014.

Weng, Helen Y., Andrew S. Fox, Alexander J. Shackman,
Diane E. Stodola, Jessica Z. K. Caldwell, Matthew C.
Olson, Gregory M. Rogers, and Richard J. Davidson. "Compassion Training Alters Altruism and Neural Responses
to Suffering." *Psychological Science* 24, no. 7 (July 2013):
1171–1180. doi: 10.1177/0956797612469537.

# INDEX

# ABOUT THE AUTHOR

**Lara Hocheiser,** E-RYT, RCYT, RCYS, YACEP, is a New York-based author, yoga and mindfulness instructor, educator, and kids' yoga and mindfulness teacher trainer. She is the founder of Flow and Grow Kids Yoga, serving students and educators worldwide with programming, curricula, and training. She has a registered children's yoga school and has trained hundreds of people since 2012. She is a mother, poet, and science fiction writer.